SO-AZO-635

This book belongs to

Rebecca

I dreamed I was
a ballerina

The Dancing Class

a girlhood story by Anna Pavlova
illustrated with art by Edgar Degas

THE METROPOLITAN MUSEUM OF ART
New York

ATHENEUM BOOKS FOR YOUNG READERS
New York · London · Toronto · Sydney · Singapore

Vivid are my earliest recollections, which take me back to the time when I was living in a little apartment with my mother in the city.

View of Saint-Valéry-sur-Somme

I was the only child; and my father having died two years after my birth, we two were alone in the world. We were very poor— very poor indeed...

and yet my mother would never fail to provide, on special occasions, a surprise for me, in the shape of some treat. I can still remember my enthusiasm when, on one birthday, I heard that we were to celebrate by going to see a performance at the theater.

At the Milliner's

1882
Degas

I had never yet been to the theater, and I plied my mother with questions in order to find out what kind of show it was that we were going to see.

She replied by telling me the story of the Sleeping Beauty—a favorite of mine among all fairy tales, and one which she had already told me countless times.

When we started for the theater, I felt
unspeakably happy beside my mother, her
arm tenderly enclosing my waist.

"You are going to enter fairyland," she said,
as we were being whirled across the darkness
toward the theater, that mysterious unknown.

The music of the *Sleeping Beauty* is by our great Tchaikovsky. As soon as the orchestra began to play, I became very grave and attentive, eagerly listening, moved for the first time in my life by the call of Beauty.

Degas

But when the curtain rose, displaying the golden hall of a wonderful palace, I could not withhold a shout of delight.

Dancer Onstage (detail)

And I remember hiding my face in my
hands when the old hag appeared on the
stage in her car driven by rats.

In the second act a swarm of youths and
maidens appeared, and danced a most
delightful waltz.

The Ballet from Robert le Diable (detail)

"How would you like to dance thus?" asked my mother with a smile.

"Oh," I replied, "I should prefer to dance as the pretty lady does who plays the part of the princess. One day I shall be the princess, and dance upon the stage of this very theater."

Dancers, Pink and Green (detail)

My mother muttered that I was her silly little dear, and never suspected that I had just discovered the idea that was to guide me throughout my life.

Little Girl Practicing at the Bar

OVERLEAF: *The Dance Class* (detail)

When we left the theater, I was living in a dream. During the journey home, I kept thinking of the day when I should make my first appearance on the stage, in the part of the Sleeping Beauty.

That very night, I
dreamed that I was a
ballerina, and spent
my whole life dancing,
like a butterfly, to the
sounds of Tchaikovsky's
lovely music.

I love to remember that
night.

The Rehearsal Onstage (detail)

Anna Pavlova in La Fille Mal Gardée

About Anna Pavlova

Born poor in a suburb of St. Petersburg, Russia, Anna Pavlova (1881–1931) was inspired to enter the ballet after seeing a performance of the *Sleeping Beauty* at the Mariinsky Theater with her mother. At the time, the public favored athletic Italian ballerinas, so young Anna's weak feet and scrawny body were not considered promising. However, after several years of practicing and waiting, Pavlova was finally admitted to the Imperial Ballet School.

Upon graduation from the school, with much ingenuity and hard work, Pavlova had begun transforming her weaknesses into gifts. She modified her ballet shoes with leather and stitching to give herself greater stamina. (Today's ballet slippers are similar to those adapted by Pavlova.) And she used her flexible body and delicate manner to give her performances an expressiveness that audiences loved.

Eventually, Pavlova became prima ballerina at the Mariinsky Theater, fulfilling her childhood dream. She toured widely throughout the world—it has been said that she journeyed 350,000 miles to 4,000 cities in fifteen years—often performing her signature piece, "The Dying Swan."

In 1931, Pavlova contracted pleurisy, an inflammation of the lungs. Doctors could have saved her life with an operation that would have left her unable to perform, but Pavlova refused to live without dancing. Her last words were reportedly "Get my swan costume ready." The night after her death, at the theater where she was to perform "The Dying Swan," the orchestra played, the curtain opened, and a spotlight went up on an empty stage.

About Edgar Degas
The French Impressionist artist Edgar Degas (1834–1917) created paintings, drawings, pastels, sculpture, and photographs. One of his favorite subjects was the ballet dancers of the Paris Opéra, who feature in about fifteen hundred of his works. Degas was as familiar with the discipline of the dancers' practice sessions as he was with the magic of their performances.

Self-portrait

Degas never worked with Anna Pavlova, and they probably never met. It is possible that he saw her perform in Paris, but that would have been decades after he created most of his ballet-inspired art. Despite their separate histories, Degas's art and Pavlova's words reveal a shared passion: the mesmerizing spell of ballet.

This story is drawn from Anna Pavlova's 1922 autobiography, *Pages of My Life* (translated by Sebastien Voirol), published by Michel de Brunoff, Paris.

The photograph of Anna Pavlova inside this book (in *La Fille Mal Gardée*, from a program, 1910) and the photograph of Pavlova on the back cover (in "The Dying Swan," ca. 1910) are from the Theater Collection of the Museum of the City of New York. All other works of art reproduced in this book are by Edgar Degas (French, 1834–1917) and are in the collections of The Metropolitan Museum of Art, unless otherwise noted.

Dancers Practicing at the Bar

COVER: *Dancer in Green* (detail). Pastel on paper, 28 x 15 in., ca. 1883. Bequest of Joan Whitney Payson, 1975 1976.201.7 *The Dancing Class.* Oil on wood, 7 3/4 x 10 5/8 in., probably 1871. H. O. Havemeyer Collection, Bequest of Mrs. H. O. Havemeyer, 1929 29.100.184 *View of Saint-Valéry-sur-Somme.* Oil on canvas, 20 x 24 in., 1896–98. Robert Lehman Collection, 1975 1975.1.167 *A Woman Ironing.* Oil on canvas, 21 3/8 x 15 1/2 in., 1873. H. O. Havemeyer Collection, Bequest of Mrs. H. O. Havemeyer, 1929 29.100.46 *At the Milliner's.* Pastel on pale gray wove paper, 30 x 34 in., 1882. H. O. Havemeyer Collection, Bequest of Mrs. H. O. Havemeyer, 1929 29.100.38 *Three Dancers Preparing for Class* (detail). Pastel on buff-colored wove paper, 21 1/2 x 20 1/2 in., after 1878. H. O. Havemeyer Collection, Bequest of Mrs. H. O. Havemeyer, 1929 29.100.558 *Dancer* (detail). Pastel, charcoal, and chalk on paper, 12 1/2 x 19 1/4 in., ca. 1880. From the Collection of Walter H. and Leonore Annenberg. *The Singer in Green.* Pastel on light blue laid paper, 23 3/4 x 18 1/4 in., ca. 1884. Bequest of Stephen C. Clark, 1960 61.101.7 *The Violinist,* study for *The Dance Lesson.* Pastel and charcoal on green paper, 15 3/8 x 11 3/4 in., ca. 1878–79. Rogers Fund, 1918 19.51.1 *Dancer Onstage* (detail). Gouache over graphite underdrawing on yellow paper, laid down on board, 7 x 9 in., ca. 1877. The Lesley and Emma Sheafer Collection, Bequest of Emma A. Sheafer, 1973 1974.356.30 *The Ballet from* Robert le Diable (detail). Oil on canvas, 26 x 21 3/8 in., 1871. H. O. Havemeyer Collection, Bequest of Mrs. H. O. Havemeyer, 1929 29.100.552 *Dancers, Pink and Green* (detail). Oil on canvas, 32 3/8 x 29 3/4 in., ca. 1890. H. O. Havemeyer Collection, Bequest of Mrs. H. O. Havemeyer, 1929 29.100.42 *Little Girl Practicing at the Bar.* Black chalk heightened with white chalk on pink laid paper, 12 1/8 x 11 1/2 in., ca. 1878–80. H. O. Havemeyer Collection, Bequest of Mrs. H. O. Havemeyer, 1929 29.100.943 *The Dance Class* (detail). Oil on canvas, 32 3/4 x 30 1/4 in., probably 1874. Bequest of Mrs. Harry Payne Bingham, 1986 1987.47.1 *The Rehearsal Onstage* (detail). Pastel over brush-and-ink drawing on cream-colored paper, laid down on bristol board and mounted on canvas, 21 x 28 1/2 in., 1874. H. O. Havemeyer Collection, Bequest of Mrs. H. O. Havemeyer, 1929 29.100.39 *Self-portrait.* Oil on paper, laid down on canvas, 16 x 13 1/2 in., possibly 1854. Bequest of Stephen C. Clark, 1960 61.101.6 *Dancers Practicing at the Bar.* Mixed media on canvas, 29 3/4 x 32 in., 1877. H. O. Havemeyer Collection, Bequest of Mrs. H. O. Havemeyer, 1929 29.100.34 BACK FLAP: *The Little Fourteen-Year-Old Dancer.* Bronze (partly tinted), cotton skirt, satin hair ribbon, wooden base, H. 37 1/2 in., 1879–81, cast in 1922. H. O. Havemeyer Collection, Bequest of Mrs. H. O. Havemeyer, 1929 29.100.370

Published by The Metropolitan Museum of Art and Atheneum Books for Young Readers

The Metropolitan Museum of Art
1000 Fifth Avenue, New York, New York 10028
212.570.3894
www.metmuseum.org

Atheneum Books for Young Readers
An imprint of Simon & Schuster Children's Publishing Division
1230 Avenue of the Americas, New York, New York 10020
www.SimonSaysKids.com

Copyright © 2001 by The Metropolitan Museum of Art

All rights reserved. No part of this publication may be reproduced or transmitted in any form or by any means, electronic or mechanical, including photocopy, recording, or any information storage or retrieval system, without permission in writing from the copyright owner and publisher.

First Edition
Printed in China
19 18 17 16 15 14 13 12 11 10 9 8 7 6

Produced by the Department of Special Publications, The Metropolitan Museum of Art:
Robie Rogge, Publishing Manager; William Lach, Editor; Anna Raff, Designer; Tatiana Ginsberg, Production Associate.
All photography by The Metropolitan Museum of Art Photograph Studio, except for photographs of Anna Pavlova, courtesy of the Museum of the City of New York.

Library of Congress Cataloging-in-Publication Data

Pavlova, Anna, 1881–1931.
I dreamed I was a ballerina : story by Anna Pavlova ; art by Edgar Degas.
p. cm.
ISBN 0-87099-988-5(MMA).—ISBN 0-689-84676-2 (Atheneum)
1. Pavlova, Anna, 1881–1931—Childhood and youth—Juvenile literature. 2. Ballerinas—Russia (Federation)—Biography—Juvenile literature. [1. Pavlova, Anna, 1881–1931—Childhood and youth. 2. Ballet dancers. 3. Women—Biography.] I. Degas, Edgar, 1834–1917, ill. II. Title.

GV1785.P3 A3 2001
792.8'028'092—dc21
[B]

2001030313